Hot stuff to Help Kids Cheer up

The Depression and Self-Esteem Workbook

Jerry Wilde, Ph.D.

SOURCEBOOKS, INC.®
NAPERVILLE, ILLINOIS

Hot Stuff
to Help Kids
Cheer Up

Published by Sourcebooks, Inc.
P.O. Box 4410, Naperville, Illinois 60567-4410
(630) 961-3900
Fax: (630) 961-2168
www.sourcebooks.com

Library of Congress Cataloging-in-Publication Data

Wilde, Jerry, 1962-
  Hot stuff to help kids cheer up : the depression and low self-esteem workbook / Jerry Wilde.
       p. cm.
  1. Depression in children--Juvenile literature. 2. Self-esteem in children--Juvenile literature. I. Title.

RJ506.D4W54 2007
618.92'8527--dc22
                                    2007012194

Printed and bound in the United States of America.
LSI 10 9 8 7 6 5 4 3 2

Contents

A Short Note to the Adults

Welcome! On behalf of the children and adolescents, I'd like to thank you for your interest in the welfare of the next generation. They need our help now more than ever. More are dropping out of school, living in poverty, and struggling with mental health issues than in previous eras. There are reasons to be optimistic because what a lot of children and adolescents *really* need is the time and attention of a caring adult (like you!). In a lot of cases, concerned counselors, educators, and parents are the best, and perhaps only, chance these kids have got.

I've tried to make this book easily understandable so students can work independently most of the time. There will undoubtedly be times when they need your assistance. There is only so much a book can accomplish. The human touch will fill in the gaps.

You'll notice that this book doesn't contain chapters in a traditional sense. Over the years, I've noticed that some adults feel pressured to finish a chapter or follow a schedule. It's easy to miss "teachable moments" that way. Please don't make that mistake. If a child isn't understanding a certain concept or mastering a skill, take the time necessary to clear up the confusion.

I also want to point out that the concepts and techniques presented are research-based and field-tested. The model presented in the book is based on cognitive-behavior therapy (CBT), which has extensive empirical evidence verifying its effectiveness in the treatment of depression. Both researchers and clinicians in the field will acknowledge that CBT has been effective with depressed children and adolescents.

I sincerely hope you find this book to be a useful resource to your professional library. If you have any questions or comments, feel free to contact me at (765) 939–8924 or info@angerchillout.com. Best of luck to you. Keep up the important work that you do!

Introduction

Thanks for deciding to check out this book. I know some of you would rather be doing just about anything other than reading this right now. In fact, I'll bet that some of you aren't actually reading. You're just sitting there with the book open, pretending to read. Yes, I know that old trick. I used it when I was in school, too. Do me a favor and really give this book a chance, because I honestly think this will be worthwhile for you. Plus, the print is *huge* and that'll make the pages fly by. What do you have to lose?

If you keep reading this book, I'll make you four promises:

1. You'll learn some important information about depression and low self-esteem.
2. You'll learn some ways to help yourself think better which will make you feel better.
3. You'll still hate doing homework.
4. You'll still like Saturdays better than Mondays.

Those last two don't have anything to do with this book, but I just wanted to let you know it'll still be a hassle to get motivated to do your homework, and Mondays will still be...Mondays! Some things never change.

Before we get going I thought you might like to know a little about me and why I wrote this book.

Name:	Jerry Wilde
Job:	College Professor
Lives In:	Indiana
Hair:	Yes
Wife:	Polly
Daughter:	Anna
Son:	Jack
Cat:	Spazmo
Dogs:	Theo and Roscoe
Favorite Bands:	(old school) AC/DC, Thin Lizzy, UFO (new school) Katatonia, Opeth, and hundreds of others
Favorite Movies:	Any movie about baseball
Hobbies:	Playing with my kids, listening to music, running, playing guitar,

Cool Things: reading, refusing to grow up
Iowa Hawkeyes, music, Diet
Mountain Dew, my family,
Minnesota Twins, Green Bay
Packers, sunny days

Uncool Things: Ignorance, wasting time,
judgmental people

I decided to write this book because I think I can help you learn the skills necessary to understand and overcome feelings of depression and low self-esteem. I've written several other books about depression, but they were for counselors and psychologists, not for students. This one is just for you.

Are you ready to hear about the hard part? You had to know there was a catch, didn't you? There's always a catch. Okay, here it is.

Since there really isn't any magic in the world, **you won't feel differently if you don't think and act differently.** Your friends, parents, teachers, dogs, cats, and gerbils can't *make* you feel better. I certainly can't magically fix your life with a book, but I can help you learn some ideas and activities that have been proven to work. To feel better you're going to have to actually do some of the things that I'll be suggesting. Your life won't suddenly be perfect, but you'll feel better.

Over the years I've worked with hundreds of students and they've had a lot of luck with the ideas I'm going to teach you. You can learn to have a happier life, but it will not be easy. If you work hard at the things in this book, you'll feel better. If you don't work hard, you probably won't. **You are totally free to choose.** But keep in mind you are also free to experience all the unhappiness your heart can bear.

Learning to "un-depress" yourself is like learning any new skill. It takes a lot of hard work and practice. There are absolutely no shortcuts, but the rewards are worth the effort.

I want you to understand the way this book is laid out. The first half of the book will be explaining important concepts about depression and low self-esteem. The last half will be spent applying what you've learned to your life. Now, it's time to get to work.

Depression in America

Depression is fairly common in children and adolescents today. That's not a good thing, but you need to realize that a lot of other students share the same kinds of feelings you are experiencing. About 2.2 million adolescents age twelve to seventeen experienced at least one major period of depression in the past year. That's nearly 10 percent of everyone in that age group.

I first got interested in this topic several years ago when I was doing research in the high school where I worked. I gave eighty high school students a depression survey called the Beck Depression Inventory. Of those eighty randomly selected high school students, 25 percent were at least mildly depressed. I was shocked that there were so many high school students suffering from depression in my little high school in Wisconsin. I became interested in learning more about the causes of depression and how I could help students who were depressed.

Why Are You Reading This Book?

My guess is one of the reasons you're reading this book is because your life isn't going as well as it could. You're upset, unhappy, or unfulfilled, which are all ways of saying that you are in some type of **pain**.

Over the years, I've thought a lot about pain, both physical and emotional. I think I have figured out one of the things pain can do for us. When things weren't going well for me, I used to wonder if I had done something to deserve it. Why was I being punished? Then I had a realization: **Pain is not intended to be a punishment. Pain is meant to teach us.** Let me explain what I mean.

When we are in physical pain, we stop doing whatever it is that's hurting us. If we pick up something hot and it burns us, we put it down. The pain is like a warning: "Hey, there's a problem here. What you're smelling is your hand burning. Put it down." Emotional pain can work the same way.

If you're depressed or suffering with low self-esteem, that pain you're feeling may be a message to change **what you're doing** and **how you're thinking**. The pain isn't sent by some evil force to ruin our lives. It's intended to teach us that we need to make some changes.

We've all put puzzles together. Sometimes we try to put a piece of the puzzle in a certain spot and it just doesn't fit. Do we try that same puzzle piece in the same spot over and over again, or do we look for a new piece? Well, if you've ever been successful with puzzles, you've recognized that when something isn't working, it's time to try something different. The same thing is true in your emotional life. If you find yourself in long-term emotional pain, often it's because the way you're thinking and behaving isn't "fitting into the puzzle." It's time to try something new.

I am not saying that every painful situation is your fault. I'm not blaming everyone who isn't happy 24/7. That would be stupid. There are times when people go through tough stuff. For example, your parents may be getting a divorce, or you may be moving away from your friends. It could be that you've had a bad breakup. There are times when life kicks our butts for a while. But I'm not talking about major traumas in your life. I'm talking about the normal, day-to-day-living stuff.

Write down some of the things that just haven't been working in your life. What situations or events have you been upset about? Are you having trouble with your friends? Are you fighting with your family? Whatever they are, write them down below.

1. _____

2. _____

3. _____

We'll come back to these later in the book, but for now, it's good to get them recorded.

Sadness or Depression?

Like I just said, most people have occasional periods of time when they're feeling "down." Life dishes out a lot of disappointment, so it's only natural that you'll feel sad from time to time. If you had a major disappointment, it would be natural to feel disappointed. Heck, you'd be *abnormal* not to be a little upset. How can you tell the difference between normal sadness and depression?

Today, people use the terms "sadness" and "depression" like they're the same thing, but they're not. Sadness is a normal emotion that everyone experiences. Depression is an illness.

Sadness is a reaction to loss, disappointment, or a significant change, and usually only lasts for a few hours or a few days. Sometimes it can go on for a longer period of time. Depression is longer lasting and much more intense than sadness. If we were going to measure the differences on a scale from 1–10, sadness would be a 3 or 4. Depression would be a 9 or 10.

Major/Clinical Depression

The most serious type of depression is called *major depression* or *clinical depression*. It's serious—it interferes with your life, and some students who suffer from major depression feel so bad that they may even try to commit suicide. Experts estimate that most periods of major depression last between seven and nine months. Telling the difference between normal sadness and clinical depression isn't easy. There isn't a magical test doctors can use. There isn't a certain type of symptom that lets us know with 100 percent certainty that people are clinically depressed. It's more important to determine if the symptoms are a change from the way they normally act and feel.

Here's a list of the most common symptoms of major or clinical depression. Put an X next to the ones that are true for you.

- [ ] Feelings of worthlessness, anxiety, emptiness, irritability, and/or hopelessness
- [ ] loss of interest in activities, hobbies, or relationships
- [ ] reduced pleasure in daily activities
- [ ] inability to enjoy activities which used to be

sources of pleasure

☐ change in appetite (usually a loss of appetite but sometimes an increase)

☐ change in weight (unintentional weight loss or unintentional weight gain)

☐ persistent difficulty falling asleep or staying asleep (insomnia)

☐ excessive daytime sleepiness

☐ fatigue

☐ difficulty concentrating or making decisions

☐ memory difficulties

☐ acting-out behavior (missing curfews, unusual defiance)

☐ *thoughts about suicide

☐ *plans to commit suicide or actual suicide attempt

*If you put an X next to either of the last two, please talk to someone **immediately**. Tell your parents, call a friend, or talk to a teacher—but tell someone. If you feel that you can't talk to anyone you know, you can always pick up the phone. Here's the number of a toll-free hotline: 1–800–SUICIDE (1–800–784–2433).

Suicide is **not** the answer. **Suicide is a permanent solution to a temporary problem.** Suicide is like junking a great car because it has a flat tire. Sure, the tire is flat now, but that can be changed. Killing yourself is like throwing away your favorite jeans because they got dirty. They may be dirty now, but they won't stay that way. Life may seem hopeless, but things have a way of working out. You have to hang in there through the tough times.

Just because you put an X next to some of the symptoms above doesn't necessarily mean you're depressed. Here are three important questions to ask:

1. Are the symptoms a change from the way you normally act and feel?

   Yes   No

2. Have you had the symptoms for an extended period of time (at least two weeks)?

   Yes   No

3. Are the symptoms interfering with your life?

   Yes   No

If the answer to these three questions is yes, you could be suffering from major depression. If this is true for you, my hope is that you're already seeing a counselor of some kind. If you're not getting some kind of help, I'm going to ask you to do me a favor. I'm going to ask you to be **brave** and tell someone that you need help. People have funny ideas about asking for help. They think it means they're weak, but they've got it backward. The people who think it's brave to suffer in silence are wrong. They're too scared to ask for help. What's brave about that? The brave ones are the people who ask for help.

Dysthymia

Dysthymia has many of the same symptoms as major depression, but the symptoms are less intense. Most students who have dysthymia can function in their day-to-day lives, but everything seems to take longer and is harder to complete. It's like you're in slow motion.

One of the ways dysthymia differs from major depression is that it tends to hang on and on and on! Major depression tends to last, on average, between seven and nine months, but dysthymia can last for years. Experts believe that the average length of dysthymia is four years. Sometimes students have felt this way for so long they no longer realize they feel bad!

A majority of students (about 70 percent) who have dysthymia will eventually develop major depression. That's why it's important to deal with the problem now before it gets any worse.

Here's a list of the common symptoms associated with dysthymia. Like before, put an X next to the ones that are true for you.

- ☐ tiredness
- ☐ very little energy
- ☐ negativity about almost everything
- ☐ hopelessness
- ☐ irritability or anger a lot of the time
- ☐ acting-out behavior
- ☐ changes in sleep patterns (either too much or too little)
- ☐ difficulty concentrating

Bipolar Disorder

Another type of depression is *bipolar disorder* or *manic depression*, which is a combination of major depression and "mania," a condition associated with feelings of high energy, extreme happiness, and confidence. It's called bipolar ("bi" as in "two," like the tires on a bike) because it's almost like having two different conditions, the depression and the mania.

When students are depressed, they experience the same feelings I've already described. When they're in a manic phase, they'll have feelings of high energy, extreme happiness, and confidence. Students who are in a manic phase often report that they have racing thoughts (thoughts going a million miles an hour) and have no need for sleep.

Students with bipolar disorder go back and forth between being depressed and being manic. Sometimes the cycles take months and other times they switch back and forth several times a day.

Causes of Depression

Depression is such a royal pain. It makes it hard to do the simplest things. Getting out of bed in the morning is a huge task for some people struggling with depression.

Before anyone can help you learn how to cope with depression, it's a good idea to understand where it comes from. What the heck causes people to feel so bad?

The truth is nobody is 100 percent certain why some people get depressed and others do not. That's because there's more than one reason people become depressed. For example, some people have a history of depression in their families. If their parent(s) suffered from depression, it's more likely that they will have to deal with this illness. Some students may have slight differences in the way a part (or parts) of their brains works and that is probably why they become depressed. Other people have a "mindset" or way of thinking about the world that leads to depression. Sometimes people have a combination of family history, brain chemical differences, and mindset problems. All of these factors are associated with depression and are more common in children and adolescents who suffer from depression. Let's examine these three in more detail.

Family/Genetic Factors

Between 20 and 50 percent of depressed students

have one or more family members who have suffered from depression in the past. In fact, if your parent(s) have been clinically depressed, you are three times more likely to experience depression than if your parents are "normal." (Well, nobody has "normal parents," but you know what I mean—if your parents haven't been depressed.) What's important to remember is that even if your parent(s) have been depressed, there is still at least a 50 percent chance that you *won't* become depressed.

Biological/Brain Factors

Some of the symptoms of depression include biological changes, such as differences in appetite and sleep, which make experts think that there are biological or brain factors related to depression. In depressed adults, there are changes in a system that produces brain chemicals known as *neurotransmitters*. Experts believe that these same changes are present in depressed children. We'll look into this in more detail a little later in the book.

Recently, the National Institute of Mental Health conducted a large experiment on the treatment of teenage depression. This study is known as

Treatment for Adolescents with Depression Study, or TADS for short.

TADS studied a type of "talking therapy" known as cognitive behavior therapy, medication, and a combination of both. Talking therapy is just what it sounds like. Students talk to a counselor who tries to help them feel better. The study used 439 teenagers (both male and female) ages twelve to seventeen at a dozen different sites in the United States.

The researchers reported that a combination of talking therapy and medication was the most effective treatment. 71 percent of the teenagers who received both treatments improved. Over 60 percent of the adolescents who received medication (Prozac) alone also improved. Finally, the "talking therapy" also helped, with 34.8 percent reporting improvement.

So the best results were from a combination of talking therapy and medication. Some students really hate the idea of taking a pill each day, and I understand that. But if that's what it takes to feel better, why not? Let me put it this way: would you rather feel bad, or take a pill the size of a Skittle and probably feel better? That's an easy choice for me, especially if you have a medical problem that's making you feel bad. When you have a medical problem, it makes sense to use medicine to get better.

A few years ago, my kidneys stopped working. I was young and healthy, but I had a nasty disease that basically "killed" my kidneys. I spent almost two years having my blood cleaned by having it sucked out of my body, spun around in a machine, and pumped back into me. This treatment, known as dialysis, lasted about ten hours each week and involved lots and lots of needles. Plus, I felt terrible…tired, sick, no appetite, couldn't sleep, etc.

I had a medical problem that was going to kill me unless I got a medical solution. I was lucky enough to have a kidney transplant, so now I no longer have to: 1) feel sick, 2) have giant needles shoved into my arms three times a week, or 3) sit in a chair for hours a week watching my blood get sucked out of me. Gross, I know! All I have to do now is take medicine to keep healthy. And let me tell you, I take a lot of medicine! I had a medical problem and I needed a medical solution. Do I mind taking medicine every day? Heck no! Are you kidding me? So I ask you, what's the big deal about taking medicine if a doctor believes it's going to help you? Write your answer below:

1. _____

2. _____

3. _____

One more thing before we move on. As I said earlier, the results of TADS show that the *best* results are from a combination of medication and cognitive behavior therapy. That means you've got to do your part, too. That "part" includes working on the things I'm going to teach you and doing the practice.

Mindset/Thinking Factors

Last but not least is the fact that certain ways of thinking about the world are related to depression and self-esteem problems. A guy named Aaron Beck noticed that some people go through tough events and don't get depressed. They may be unhappy and they certainly aren't whistling *Yankee Doodle Dandy*, but they aren't depressed. He wondered, *What's the difference between the people who face bad things and only get sad, and the folks who go through the same type of stuff and get depressed or even suicidal?* He started studying depression and he's never stopped. That was forty years ago!

Okay, pay close attention here because this next part is really important. Dr. Beck concluded that it *wasn't* the bad events that caused depression. It was the person's thoughts, beliefs, and attitudes *about* the events that were responsible for the depression. And that is fantastic news. If thoughts cause depression, it means people can learn how to change those thoughts so they don't get depressed or don't stay that way. If it were the events or "bad things" that caused depression, we'd all be completely powerless. We'd have no freedom, no control—we'd be like puppets.

Dr. Beck eventually figured out that there are three basic beliefs that lead to depression. He referred to these three beliefs as the "cognitive triad."

1. Negative View of the Self

Most beliefs related to depression start with the basic idea, "I am no good. I'm worthless and unlovable." People who have this belief talk to themselves and their "self-talk" sounds like:

"I am no good and will never amount to anything."

"I deserve the bad treatment I get."

"No matter what I do I will fail."

"I can't do anything right."

"Nobody could ever love me because I am worthless."

How could people feel anything but depressed if they walked around with these messages inside their heads all day long? These messages play over and over again like a CD. When people hear themselves saying, "I'm a no-good, unlovable jerk," they become more and more convinced that the message is true.

2. Negative View of the World

Not only do a lot of depressed students feel *they* are hopeless, many feel the *world* is hopeless as well. They seem to think the problems of the world are beyond repair.

"You have to watch your back because people are out to take advantage of you."

"Any day now, the world is going to end. It can't go on like this."

It isn't hard to understand how people could start to believe that the world is a terrible place. It is nearly impossible to turn on a television without being bombarded with bad news. We can't lose sight of the fact that while there are many bad things that occur in the world, there are also lots of things to be happy about. I am grateful for so many things and I remind myself every single day that no matter what happens there are things I will be enjoying the rest of my life. For example, I love music and always find pleasure in it, whether it's listening to it or frightening my pets while I blast away on my guitar. Nothing can ever change that.

Take a moment and write down three things that help you feel happiness that can't be taken away from you.

1. _____

2. _____

3. _____

I know this sounds like something your grandma would tell you, but if you focus on the things that bring you happiness instead of the things that bring you down, you'll feel better. Your thoughts largely control how you feel, and *you* control your thoughts.

3. Negative View of the Future

Sometimes people believe that the bad things they are currently experiencing will last forever. That's obviously a depressing thought. Some look into the future and see nothing but problems and more difficulties.

"I'll never get over this."

"I can't change the horrible things that have happened to me in the past so I'm doomed forever."

"There is no way out."

"Life sucks now and will always suck."

Low Self-Esteem

Another topic that will be addressed in this book is low self-esteem. In some ways it is like depression, but in other ways it isn't, because low self-esteem doesn't appear to have the biological/brain factors mentioned earlier. It is similar to depression in that low self-esteem tends to be associated with the mindset/thinking patterns we just covered.

People who have low self-esteem basically have a low opinion of themselves. Another way to say this is that they don't care enough about themselves. They think that they are too fat, too skinny, too tall, too short; that their hair is ugly; or that their family isn't right. The list could go on and on. My experience working with students leads me to believe that it usually comes down to two or three issues: their appearance, their friends/popularity, or whether they have a boyfriend or girlfriend.

There are other factors that affect self-esteem, and let's take a minute to get you to think about how you feel about each *right now* and *how you'd like to feel.* Write down a number between 1 and 10 for each entry below.

	How I Feel Now	How I'd Like to Feel
Appearance	_____	_____
Boyfriend/Girlfriend	_____	_____
Family	_____	_____
Friends	_____	_____
Popularity	_____	_____
Grades	_____	_____

I don't want you to think that I believe appearances are completely unimportant. There are real advantages to having a nice appearance, and there's nothing wrong with *wanting* to look good. But there are a lot of students who are *overly* concerned about their appearance. They place too much attention on their looks. They think there is something about the way they look that makes them a "freak." Some people have classmates who tease them, and that certainly doesn't help.

If you are struggling with low self-esteem because you aren't happy with your appearance, I'd like you to consider another way of thinking about the situation. Let's say that you have low self-esteem because you don't like the way you look. You think you *know* that everyone is laughing at you because of your freakish appearance. I'd like to consider this:

I'm convinced no one is obsessing about your appearance (except you!)

That's right—my belief is that *no one* is obsessing about your appearance. That's because **all your classmates are obsessing about their own appearances.** You think they're looking at you and your: a) enormous zit, b) weird haircut, or c) tiny ears, etc., but they're not. They're actually thinking about themselves.

Another common reason students have low self-esteem is because they don't have a boyfriend or a girlfriend. Most of your friends seem to have found someone special, but you haven't, so you think it means you're unlovable. It doesn't. Once again, try considering another idea.

Whether or not you have a boyfriend or a girlfriend really has more to do with the people around you. Maybe there isn't a good match for you. Maybe the time isn't right. Maybe you haven't met anyone special yet.

Here's a very weird example that might help you think about it differently. Some people don't have a puppy. Does that mean they'll never have one? It could be because the time isn't right. Maybe you haven't found your type of puppy yet. Just because you haven't got a puppy doesn't mean you're unlovable or that you'll never have one. In fact, if one of your friends came up to you and said, "I don't have a puppy. That must mean I'm unlovable," you'd think your friend had lost his or her mind! Why would you believe you're unlovable just because you don't have a boyfriend or girlfriend? Like I said, a lot of times that has to do with circumstances beyond your control.

One more thought before we move on: why does having a boyfriend or girlfriend *make* you worthwhile? Does it make you smarter? Cooler? Cuter? Nope. Having a boyfriend or girlfriend doesn't change anything about you. It doesn't make you taller (or shorter). It doesn't make your hair curlier (or straighter). You're still you. Nothing about you has changed either way, and it doesn't *prove* anything about you. It's more about the person you're with than about you.

Self-Esteem Insanity

One of the things that has always bugged me about self-esteem has to do with the way some people think about it. Some people believe that you deserve to feel good about yourself *only* when you have done something worthwhile. It's like you're required to *earn* your self-esteem. People seem to think you're not supposed to feel good about yourself just because you're alive.

A tremendous amount of emotional suffering is caused by the idea that you can only accept yourself when you have achieved something worthwhile. Let me explain how the current ideas about self-esteem have caused millions of students to feel they are less than they *should* be.

If people believe they are only worthwhile when they are successful, they will always have a tendency to feel uptight. This is due to the possibility that they might fail at something they believe to be important. Every new test, new assignment, new game, and new day will be viewed as a threat because they believe they *have* to succeed. This nagging anxiety will be there even when things are going fine.

What happens when they don't succeed? If they believe they're supposed to feel proud of themselves *only* when they do well, they'll probably also think they should feel bad about themselves when they fail. That's the way the self-esteem teeter-totter works. These crazy ideas about self-esteem have set them up to be miserable. They can't win. If they do well, they'll feel good about themselves but they'll still be uptight. If they fail, they'll feel like failures!

There's another problem with this "self-esteem insanity." It confuses "success" with "self-worth."

Think of it this way: most people would agree that being successful is enjoyable. Who doesn't like to do well or win the game or get a good grade? But simply because you were fortunate enough to experience something enjoyable does not mean you *should* feel good about yourself.

Eating pizza is enjoyable, but if you had the chance to eat your favorite kind of pizza, you wouldn't feel proud of yourself. You certainly wouldn't feel badly about yourself if you didn't get to eat pizza. You might feel hungry but you certainly wouldn't think, "I'm a loser because I didn't eat pizza." The crazy ideas about self-esteem seem to be saying, "If you succeed (which is enjoyable) you can feel good about yourself. If you fail, you should feel like a loser." That's just plain crazy. **Don't equate how well you do with your self-worth.**

Your accomplishments are not a reflection of your value, just a measure of your performance in something. Academic grades, good or bad, can't make you any more or less worthwhile. Doing great in sports (or doing poorly in sports) isn't a measure of *you*. It's a measure of how well you do in sports, which is only one tiny *part* of you.

My hero, Albert Ellis, said that having high self-esteem is just a fancy way of saying you're not *too* concerned with what other people think of you. And you know what? He's right. I'm not saying you should be arrogant. I'm just saying it doesn't make sense to let other people determine how you feel about yourself. Seriously, why does it matter what other people think of you? Their opinion of you is a reflection of *them*. It really doesn't say much about you.

If you have low self-esteem, it usually means you're overly concerned with others' opinions of you. In other words, you're probably overly self-conscious.

What parts of your life are you self-conscious about? Is it your physical appearance? Your clothes? Your social life? Boyfriend or girlfriend? Popularity? Write down up to three things below.

1. _____
2. _____
3. _____

Okay, I want you to really think about this next question. Why does it matter? You've got funny ears, a big nose, or a big butt? So what! (Hey, that kind of rhymed). Seriously, does that prove you are a bad person or that somehow you *should* feel bad about yourself? Once you start to accept yourself (with your big nose), you'll feel better.

Write down how worrying about other people's opinions of you is making your life better. How is it helping you?

1. _____

2. _____

3. _____

There are very few advantages. What it *does* do for you is make you unhappy and uptight.

Now write down how worrying about other people's opinions of you is making your life worse.

1. _____

2. _____

3. _____

This is a losing battle because you can't control what other people think of you. You *can* control how much you're going to buy into their beliefs. You *can* develop self-confidence. All you have to do is accept yourself and like yourself for who you are, not who others want you to be.

Mindset Factors (Again)

Earlier there was a section of the book that described ideas that tend to be associated with depression. Aaron Beck said that depressed people tend to believe one or more of the following thoughts:

1. "I'm no good." (negative view of self)
   Yes   No
2. "The world stinks." (negative view of the world)
   Yes   No
3. "The future will be horrible." (negative view of future)
   Yes   No

My question for you is, "Do you believe any of these three ideas (negative view of self, world, or future)?" It's okay to be honest.

If you answered "yes," describe which one(s) you believe and why?

_____

_____

_____

This next part might be tough but I want you to

really think about this question: How did you come to believe these idea(s)? What started you believing it?

_____

_____

_____

It's very important that you learn to listen to your thinking (also called "self-talk"). Remember, it's largely thoughts that cause depression (and all the other emotions, too). Most people believe that events cause emotions. For example, most students (and teachers) think that other people or bad events *cause* emotions, but that's not true. Are you convinced that the way you think *causes* you to feel what you feel? (circle one)

Yes   No

I wouldn't be surprised if you circled "no." That's fine. Let me tell you a story designed to prove it to you.

Let's say it's a normal afternoon at your school. You're walking down the hall and all of a sudden someone knocks your books out of your hands. The books go flying and some of the other students start kicking your books down the hall. How would you **feel** after getting your books knocked out of your hands?

I'd feel _____

Most students write down that they'd be mad or even scared after having their books scattered.

What would you be **thinking** to yourself after your books were knocked out of your hands?

I'd think _____

A lot of people say that they'd be thinking something like, "People should be more careful" or "People should watch what they're doing."

Now you turn around, feeling sort of mad (or scared), wondering what they heck this student's problem is and then you realize that he's blind. He's a blind student who is new to your school and he *accidentally* bumped into you. **Now** how would you feel?

_____

I'm willing to bet you wouldn't be angry anymore. Most students say they'd feel sad because they were mad at this student who accidentally bumped into them. Others say they'd feel a sense of pity for him.

How would your thoughts change when you realized it was an accident and that he didn't mean to bump into you? In other words, what would you be thinking once you realized it was an accident?

_____

People often say they would be thinking something like, "He didn't mean to do it" or "It's no big deal. It was an accident."

Here's the important part. The event (getting your books knocked out of your hands) stayed the same. Your feelings changed *after* your thoughts changed. If events *caused* feelings, how could the same event (getting your books knocked out of your hands) cause different feelings? It couldn't, could it? When your thoughts changed from something like, "He should be more careful" to thoughts such as, "It was an accident," your feelings changed too. **It was your thoughts that caused you to feel what you felt.** Once again, that's great news because we can learn to change our thoughts. We can't control other people or things but we can learn to control what goes on between our ears. It's called cognitive-behavior therapy.

Now for Some More Good News

Cognitive-behavior therapy (CBT) is the type of counseling that helps students listen to what they are thinking and decide if their thoughts are true or false. It's a system that challenges people to think rational or true thoughts about themselves and their world.

What you need to understand is that **you feel how you think**. I know that sounds weird but it's true. If you think the world stinks and that you're a gigantic loser, of course you're going to have low self-esteem or feel depressed. That only makes sense. **If you think depressing thoughts, you'll probably feel depressed**. You are going to *feel* pretty much whatever you *think*. You *can* learn to:

1. Hear what you're thinking,
2. Check if your thoughts are true or false, and
3. If they are false, change them to something that's true.

While this is simple to say, it's a heck of a lot harder to do. Let's start by clarifying the importance of thoughts and feelings.

Thoughts and Feelings

For the people who still need more convincing that thoughts and feelings are connected, let me give you some more *proof*. As we'll learn later, it's usually a good idea to look for proof. I don't think it's wise to believe anything just because somebody told you it was so.

Below is a list of thoughts. Your job is to decide which feeling would probably go with each thought. My guess is you'll be able to do this pretty easily. Why? Because thoughts influence feelings. If they didn't, your answers would be totally different from your friends', but I'll bet they'll be mostly the same. Give this a try and see how it goes.

What type of *feeling* would you have if you thought:

"Oh, no....I didn't know there was a test today."

Feeling_____

"What do you mean I'm grounded?"

Feeling_____

"I'm worthless."

Feeling_____

"It's not fair that I got a detention from Mr. Jones."
Feeling_____
"Life stinks."
Feeling_____
"I found a ten dollar bill as I was walking down the street."
Feeling_____
"My mom and dad are having an argument."
Feeling_____

See, that wasn't hard to do, was it? Once you know the thought, attaching the feeling to it is easy. Here's one more thing you can do if you still doubt the connection between thoughts and feelings.

Right now, *have a feeling without having a thought.* Go ahead and try to have a feeling without thinking about anything at all.

You can't do it, can you? Feelings come from thoughts. Events don't cause feelings. If you're still not convinced, I'll try one more idea.

Same Event, Different Feelings

Do the same events cause the same feelings in people? For example, if one hundred people had the exact same experience, would they all feel the same way? Probably not, but let's use an example to clarify this point.

Let's say that one hundred people got a math test back and received a grade of C+. Would everyone feel the same way? I doubt it. Some students would be bummed out ("I got a C+. My folks are going to kill me"). Others would be happy ("Dude, I got a C+ which means I finally passed a math test"). **They'd feel differently because they'd think differently**.

Events are neutral until we think about them and give them meaning. Seriously. To prove this to you I'm going to write down something that most people would consider a "bad event" and your job is to write down a thought that would bring about a happy feeling.

Event: You got a Saturday detention

What thought could you have that would make a Saturday detention a happy experience?

_____

_____

_____

Most students write down one of two thoughts. They usually say, "Well, at least I'd get out of my chores" or "I'd get to hang out with my friends."

Some say, "At least I'd get caught up on homework."

Okay, the new event is the reverse. This time I'm going to write down something that most people would consider a "good event" and your job is to write down a thought that would bring about unhappy feelings.

Event: You just won the lottery for $100,000,000

What thought could you have that would make winning the lottery an unhappy experience?

_____

_____

_____

I've had students write that they'd be afraid people would like them just for their money or they'd be worried they might get kidnapped.

So once again, events don't cause feelings. Beliefs, ideas, and thoughts cause feelings and if you change your thoughts, you'll change your feelings. Now that you have a better understanding of the connection between thoughts and feelings, let's move on.

True or False?

The next important step is learning to tell if a thought is true or false. It makes sense that you want to tell yourself the truth. Why would you want to walk around believing something that isn't true?

The best way to determine if a thought is true or false is to use the same methods scientists use when they're doing experiments. Scientists only believe ideas if they can *prove* them to be true. What I want you to do is examine your thinking to find out if your ideas are true. If you're depressed or have low self-esteem I can almost guarantee you that you're thinking thoughts that are untrue.

A good practice exercise is "Where's the Proof?" Give it a try.

Where's the Proof?

In the blank space in front of each belief, make a "T" if the belief is true and an "F" if the belief is false.

_____ 1. I don't like it when I do poorly but it's not the worst thing in the world.

_____ 2. Life has to be fair all the time.

_____ 3. If people don't like me I can still like myself.

_____ 4. I can't stand losing at something important.

_____ 5. I wish things were easier in school but they don't have to be.

_____ 6. Other people make me feel bad.

_____ 7. If I make a mistake once I will probably always make that mistake.

_____ 8. Because math is hard for me it proves I'm a stupid person.

_____ 9. If someone thinks I'm a nerd, I'm a nerd.

_____10. No matter what you say or do to me, I'm still a worthwhile person.

_____11. When things don't go the way I want, it's the worst thing ever.

_____12. I have to be right 100 percent of the time.

_____13. Things should go my way most of the time.

_____14. For the most part, I can control how I feel.

Answer key:

True - 1, 3, 5, 10, 14

False - 2, 4, 6, 7, 8, 9, 11, 12, 13

Most people tell themselves things that aren't true some of the time. For example, have you ever thought, "I know what they are saying about me?" If you've had that thought, there's a pretty good chance you were thinking something that wasn't true. Can you really read other people's minds? The answer is a big, fat "No." Sometimes we like to think we're psychic, but we're not. Let's do one more exercise that focuses on making sure you can tell the difference between true and false beliefs.

True vs. False Beliefs

Directions: Next to each statement, write "T" if the belief is true and "F" if the belief is false.

_____ 1. I wish I could have a new stereo.

_____ 2. If I don't do as well as I would have liked on a math test, it doesn't mean I'm a stupid person.

_____ 3. My parents never let me go anywhere.

_____ 4. I don't like some subjects as much as others but I can stand them anyway.

_____ 5. If I don't get asked to the prom, I'll die.

_____ 6. If I wear these old shoes, everyone will make fun of me.

_____ 7. I wish things would be easier but they don't have to be.

_____ 8. I would prefer it if my parents would let me

stay out later.

_____ 9. If a teacher gets mad at me I don't have to get down on myself.

_____ 10. If I didn't get on the honor roll I couldn't show my face around here.

_____ 11. Even if I look like a fool it doesn't mean I am a fool.

_____ 12. People ought to treat me with the respect I deserve.

Step three is where you try changing a thought that is false into something that is true. When you think of a new thought ask yourself, "Can I prove this to be true?" If you have proof, it's probably a true thought. If you don't have proof, it's probably not true.

Changing the Thought

Underneath each false statement, write a true belief. Change the statement into something that is true.

1. Life has to treat me the way I want to be treated.

_____

_____

_____

2. I can't take it when things don't go my way.

_____

_____

_____

3. He doesn't have the right to say that to me.

_____

_____

_____

4. You have to help me because it is hard to do alone.

_____

_____

_____

5. Things never go my way.

_____

_____

_____

6. My classmates have to take my advice.

_____

_____

_____

7. My grades had better be good or I'll be a complete
   loser.

_____

_____

_____

8. It would be terrible, awful, and horrible if I didn't get my way.

_____

_____

_____

Looking Inside

Now, here's the most important part of the book. I want you to find what you are saying to yourself when you feel depressed. Remember the three ideas known as the "cognitive triad."

1. Negative view of self,
2. Negative view of world, and
3. Negative view of future.

When you are feeling depressed or having feelings of low self-esteem, there are thoughts involved. It's very important that you "hear" those thoughts. What are you saying to yourself? Write it down below.

_____

_____

_____

Sometimes students say more than one thing to themselves. Be sure to write down **all** the negative thoughts you hear.

Now, ask yourself a very important question about your thoughts from above: **Can I prove that those thoughts are true?** Notice I didn't say, "Can I prove that I believe them?" or "Can I prove that other people say those things to me?" or "Can I prove that other people believe them?" That's not the question. Can you prove those thoughts to be true?

Yes   No

If you can prove the thoughts to be true, you'll have evidence. Write down your evidence or proof that the beliefs are true.

_____

_____

_____

If you wrote, "I *really* believe them," that is not proof. If you wrote, "People tell me that all the time," that's not proof.

Let's be scientists for a minute. What do scientists do

when they have no proof that a theory or belief is true? *They throw it out.* And if you have no proof for your beliefs, that's what I want you to do, too. Throw them out. Kick 'em to the curb! Get them out of your head.

Do not lie to yourself. People lie to us enough. We don't need to lie to ourselves. But if you are walking around telling yourself something that isn't true, you are lying to yourself. Don't do that.

Alligator Thoughts

Sometimes students write down beliefs they think are causing them to feel bad *and* the beliefs have proof. For example, if you feel depressed or have low self-esteem because you think to yourself, "I don't have a lot of friends" or "I'm unpopular," that could be a true belief. We could prove those ideas to be true, right? If you can find evidence/proof for a belief that is causing you to feel depressed, that means there are probably *alligator thoughts* swimming around your brain. Alligator thoughts are the kind of ideas that float around just below the surface so you can't find them. They're in there but they're hiding.

For example, the idea "I'm unpopular" may be true, so I *know* that isn't what is causing your upset feelings. There must be an alligator thought that goes along with the original belief. For example, you might be thinking, "I'm not popular (possibly true) and that means *I'm an unlovable, rotten person* (alligator thought)." A true belief, one that you can prove, won't make you feel depressed. There's usually an alligator thought swimming right beside the true thought. If you wrote down thoughts that were causing you to feel depressed and you have proof for those thoughts, look for alligator thoughts. They're in there just below the water.

Let's do one more example. You could have written down a thought like, "I never get invited to parties." This may be true, although I doubt you *never* get invited to parties. It's probably more true that you don't get invited to the parties you'd like to get invited to. But either way the belief that "I never get invited to parties" couldn't make you feel depressed. There's an alligator thought along with it. See if you can find the gator and write it down below.

"I never get invited to parties and that means

_____."

It's probably something like, "I never get invited to parties and that means I'm uncool, a loser, etc." Is it true that because someone doesn't get invited to parties that the person is uncool? Not at all. I used to know a lot of students who didn't get invited to parties because they chose not to drink or do drugs. That didn't make them uncool. Some students didn't get invited because they were involved in so many things that they didn't have time to go to parties. Those students were some of the coolest people I knew.

Distraction

The goal of this book is to help you learn how to: 1) **stop** depressing thoughts before they drag you down and 2) **break out** of a depressed mood when you're there. There are things you can do if you notice you are starting to feel depressed. One of the best is called *distraction*.

Distraction works by thinking of something *other than* those depressing thoughts that are running around your head. But you know what happens? When you're getting depressed the *only* thing you seem to be able to think about is the person or situation that's bugging you. It's sort of like when you're really hungry, food is the only thing on your mind. That's why you need to decide what to think about *before* you start getting depressed.

You need to pick a scene to think about before you need it. This memory should be either the happiest or funniest thing you can remember. For example:

- The time you said something funny and your friend laughed so hard that milk came out of his or her nose.
- The time you got a great present for Christmas.
- Your best birthday party ever.
- The time you had an unexpected day off from school because of snow or ice.

I use a scene from a few years ago when my cat, Spazmo, tried to steal a hot dog off the kitchen table. At the time, Spazmo was a little kitten and the hot dog was almost as big as she was. Spazmo was dragging it across the floor like the hot dog was a tree!

Every time I imagine Spazmo doing battle with that hot dog I crack up laughing. There is no way I could be sad when I think about that scene.

Speaking of "milk out of noses," I also think of a time when a friend of mine had milk rocket out of both of his nostrils because someone cracked a joke just as he was swallowing. That was years and years ago but it still cracks me up every time I think of it. Thanks Kirk!

Take a few minutes and think about your distraction scene then write it down below.

_____

_____

_____

Make certain you've picked a good scene because it is important. Now you need to practice imagining this scene several times a day for the next few days. When you're sitting on the bus or waiting in line to eat lunch just close your eyes and picture your scene as clearly as you can. Bring in all the details that you can possibly remember.

- What were the people wearing?
- What were the sounds around you?

• Were there any smells in the air?

Try to make the scene in your mind just like watching a video.

The idea then is to switch to this scene when you find yourself starting to feel down. Instead of thinking about a problem, concentrate on your distraction scene. Instead of feeling sad because your friends blew you off, concentrate on your scene until you start to feel better. Whenever you feel yourself getting sad and depressed, remember to switch to your distraction scene.

You can't think of your distraction scene and still be depressed. Since feelings are produced by thoughts, if you change those thoughts to something funny or happy, it will keep you from getting upset. It will buy you time to handle it. That few seconds of time could be the difference between handling a situation and getting majorly bummed.

Right now, think back to a situation where you "depress yourself." I know that sounds weird but I used that phrase on purpose. Notice I didn't write, "Think back to a situation that *depresses you*." The situation doesn't depress you. You depress yourself about the situation. Big difference! Replay that scene in your mind and feel upset about it just like you did when it happened. Once you're feeling sad, switch to your distraction scene and focus on it like a laser. Keep focusing on your distraction scene. Now, what happened to your sadness? It's gone, isn't it?

Another Idea

This is another technique called rational-emotive imagery, which is similar to the distraction technique. It works best for people who seem to have a "trigger" for feelings of low self-esteem and depression. What I mean by trigger is that there are certain events or situations that "trigger" negative thinking. You start to get bummed out when certain things occur. It could be with a certain friend or family member or it could be with an old boyfriend or girlfriend.

Here's what you do: Close your eyes and imagine the trigger scene very clearly. Pretend you are actually there in your mind. See all the things going on in that scene. Hear the sounds that would be around you and everything about the situation. Make it as real as possible in your mind.

The next step is to feel slightly depressed for a short time. Go ahead and recapture some of the feelings of sadness just like you would if it were real life. Let yourself feel slightly depressed for ten to twenty seconds.

The next step is to make yourself feel better. Instead of thinking about the trigger situation, concentrate on making yourself feel better. Imagine a picture in your mind or focus on a positive thought to make yourself feel happier. Instead of being depressed, change your thoughts to make yourself feel better. Stay in that scene in your mind but keep working until you're able to change how you feel. When you get to the point where you've gotten yourself feeling better, take a deep breath and open up your eyes. Now, write down exactly what you thought to make yourself feel better.

_____

_____

_____

If you were able to cheer yourself up, chances are you have just written down a true belief. Look at the belief you just wrote down and ask yourself:

1. Can I prove the belief to be true?
   Yes   No

2. Is the belief most likely to bring about positive results?

    Yes   No

3. Is the belief likely to get me into or out of trouble?
Into trouble   Out of trouble

Once you've determined the belief is true, **repeat** the same practice exercise everyday. In fact, it's better to repeat this several times a day if you can. Practice thinking the true belief you've just recorded when you are trying to feel better. Write it down on a small card and carry it with you for times when you feel yourself beginning to get depressed. You can use your *distraction scene* until you are calmer. Then practice this new thought. It sounds too simple to work but it does.

Exercise and Depression

There is getting to be more and more evidence that exercise is an effective part of the treatment for depression. One experiment with adult patients compared two different ways to treat depression:

1. antidepressant medication

2. exercise

The researchers found that the people taking medication responded
sooner than the adults who were just
exercising, but after sixteen weeks,
there was no difference between the two
groups. In other words, exercise worked as
well as medication in relieving feelings of depression.

The key to exercise as a depression reliever is in a
brain chemical called phenylethylamine, or PEA,
which is a natural stimulant produced by the body.
People who are depressed tend to have low PEA levels.
Exercise has a natural antidepressant action by raising
these levels of PEA. Endorphins are other chemicals
responsible for improving mood after a workout.

Here's some more good news…you don't have to
be training for a marathon to get positive results
from exercise. Working out for as little as thirty minutes a day can have positive results. So right here,
right now, let's plan an exercise program.

What type of exercise could you do? Please list
three and I'll explain why I want you to list more
than one.

1. _____
2. _____
3. _____

What times of the day could you exercise? Remember, a lot of people get up 30 minutes early just to work out.

1. _____
2. _____
3. _____

Here's an important question: what excuses will you use to miss exercising? (You know, "I'm too busy," "Exercising is boring," "I'm too tried." etc.)

1. _____
2. _____
3. _____

Earlier I wanted you to write down at least three different ways you could work out because if you decide you're going to do the same thing everyday that *will* get boring. It's a good idea to switch it around.

Get Out and Have Some Fun

One of the things I've noticed about students who are depressed is that they tend to close themselves off from others. They retreat into themselves and shy away from nearly all social contact that isn't absolutely necessary. *Big mistake!*

When you feel bad, you stay away from everyone. When you stay away from everyone, your brain says, "You don't have any friends...what a loser you are!" Once you've convinced yourself that you don't have friends you stay shut up inside even more and the cycle goes on and on. That's why it's really important to get out and be around other people. Besides, it's so boring to just stay around your house.

Here are some things you can do to be social:

Go to a club meeting at your school. Most schools have plenty of different clubs and usually have something that almost everyone would find interesting. *Force yourself* to attend a club meeting.

Go to a sporting event at your school. Even if you're not a big sports fan, go anyway. Hey, at least you're out of the house.

Go for a walk and make yourself a promise that you'll try to start a conversation with at least one person you see on your walk.

Play a board game either with your family or some friends. I know, I know…you never play board games anymore. I promise you if you bust out a game of Monopoly, you'll have fun. I guarantee it!

Go bowling. *Always fun.* Even if you stink and only get a 64, it's still fun.

Call a friend you haven't talked to in awhile. Again, *make* yourself pick up the phone. While you're on the phone, make plans to go out and do something.

Start a kickball game in your neighborhood. I believe that kickball is the greatest game ever invented (other than baseball, basketball, and football). No seriously, kickball is massively cool. You really can't have a bad time playing kickball except if you're like me and *always* get the ball stuck in a tree or if you're like me and everyone kicks line drives off your face. I haven't mastered the art of "ducking" yet.

Think of a reason for a party and invite your friends and family.

"Lean on Me, When You're Not Strong"

No matter who you are or what you're going through, there are still people in your life that can be a source of strength. It may be your friends, your family, or your teachers. There *are* people who care about you. Write down three or four people who you know have got your back.

1. _____
2. _____
3. _____
4. _____

Sometimes when you're feeling down, you can forget that there are all sorts of folks who could help you. When you get depressed it can mess up your thinking to where all you see is the bad stuff in life.

Here's something I'd like you to try. Ask a few people in your life to write you a letter telling you what they like about you. I promise that you'll be amazed at what you get back. Just try it. Ask some friends, family members, teachers or anyone you trust and then sit back and prepare to be amazed.

Paper, Pen, Pin, and Back

I used to do an activity in group counseling that is similar to the idea described above except it's much more immediate. Everyone in the group would have a piece of paper pinned to the back of his or her shirt. Then everyone in the group would take turns writing positive comments about the person on the paper pinned to his or her back. There's something embarrassing about looking someone in the eye and giving him or her a compliment. I wish that wasn't true but it is. But people aren't at all uptight about *writing* those same comments on paper on the person's back.

After everyone has had a chance to write on everyone's back you need to take your papers off and read them aloud in the group. This can also be a really powerful experience. I know students who have saved their papers with positive comments for years.

You don't have to have twenty people to make this activity fun. It could just be you and your cousins or friends. Give it a try.

Medications for Depression

We've mentioned the topic of medications a few times in the book already. Feel free to skip ahead in the book if you are not on medication or if you have no interest in this topic.

Antidepressant medications focus on the brain chemicals (known as neurotransmitters) associated with your moods. It's a well established fact that depression can be caused by imbalances in these chemicals. These medications help the brain chemicals get back in balance so people feel better.

Three neurotransmitters in particular tend to be associated with depression. These brain chemicals are *serotonin, norepinephrine,* and *dopamine.* Most of the medications used to treat depressed students focus on adjusting these brain chemicals.

One type of medication, **tricyclic antidepressants**, works by slowing down the process by which the brain chemicals are reabsorbed into the brain. These medications are usually taken in pill form but are not addictive. They can have minor side effects such as dry mouth, headache, weight gain, and at times more serious things such as an irregular heart beat.

The most commonly prescribed tricyclic antidepressants are:

1. Imipramine (brand name is Tofranil)
2. Amitripytline (Elavil)
3. Nortripytline (Pamelor)
4. Clomipramine (Anafranil)

Monoamine Oxidase Inhibitors (MAOIs) work by blocking the chemical monoamine oxidase, which is a chemical that destroys other brain chemicals (neurotransmitters). So it works by keeping one chemical from destroying another chemical.

MAOIs are used to treat adults but are very rarely used with students because there are certain foods you cannot eat when you're taking them, and one of them is chocolate. A life without chocolate. No way!

Commonly used MAOIs are:

- Phenelzine (Nardil)
- Tranylcypromine (Parnate)

Selective Serotonin Reuptake Inhibitors (SSRIs) work by keeping the brain chemical serotonin from being reabsorbed into the brain tissue. If serotonin isn't reabsorbed into the brain, the level of serotonin in the fluid around nerve cells is increased.

Commonly used SSRIs are:
- Citalopram (Celexa)
- Paroxetine (Paxil)
- Sertraline (Zoloft)
- Fluoxetine (Prozac)

Minding Your Moods

It's a good idea to keep track of your moods so you can determine if there are trends to your ups and downs. Once you've charted your moods you can use this information as a type of prevention. For example, if you know that you tend to have down days on Sundays, you can make some plans to do something fun on that day so you won't have a lousy time. So for one month, keep track of your moods. Mark each day with a number from one to ten, with ten being "I've never felt better" and one being "I feel way bad." After you've collected this information for a month, look over the data and see if you can identify any trends.

Pain Revisited

At the start of the book I wrote that pain is supposed to teach us to change how we're living. I challenged you to write down some of the things that you are going to change. Always remember that life *isn't* about suffering. If you're unhappy, use your pain as a motivation to change. Write down what you've changed and how that has helped. If it hasn't helped, write down why you think things haven't improved.

1. _____
2. _____
3. _____

What Have You Learned?

We are nearing the end of the book and I'd like you to spend a couple of minutes reflecting on the lessons of this book. Sometimes it's helpful to try to sum things up so that's what I'd like you to do here.

Write down the three most important things you've learned from this book.

1. _____
2. _____
3. _____

I can predict that most of you will be at one of three points as you reach the end of the book:

1. Some will have made great progress.

You'll be well on your way to learning the skills to take control of the thoughts and behaviors that are causing you to feel bad. You've really tried the ideas that I've suggested and had success. With success comes confidence and even more motivation. In your head there is a little voice that says, "This really works. Awesome!"

2. Some will have made progress but are still struggling from time to time.

You'll understand how thoughts influence feelings but you may not have mastered the difficult task of actually changing your thinking. Hey, this isn't easy. Changing any habit is hard and modifying your thinking takes time.

That's okay. This is a skill that takes time to master. Keep up the practice and things will continue to improve. You'll need to be patient and persistent.

3. Some will have given up and won't believe it's possible to change how you feel.

This just isn't true. People can change. People do change. You can change, too.

Whenever you're learning a new skill there's a

point where that voice in your head says, "There's no way I can do this. It's hopeless." Whether you've tried to learn a musical instrument or understand a tough math concept, we've all been there. There was a time you didn't know simple addition but you know it now. There was a time when tying your shoes seemed impossible, but not any more (at least I hope not!). So don't give up. Nearly anything is possible if you want it bad enough.

I'd like to close with the words of one of my favorite authors, Albert Camus.

In the midst of winter,
I finally learned
That there was in me
An invincible summer.

I hope and pray that each of you discovers your own invincible summer. Peace.

Index

About the Author

 Jerry Wilde, Ph.D., is an associate professor of educational psychology for Indiana University East. Prior to this academic appointment, he had ten years of experience as a school psychologist where he worked with students who had emotional, behavioral, and learning difficulties. Dr. Wilde has written the following books:

Defying the Defiance: 131 Insights, Strategies, Activities, and Lessons for Helping Students with ODD (Oppositional Defiant Disorder) (2004) with Mike Paget and Tip Frank

Peace in the Halls: Stories and Activities to Manage Anger and Prevent School Violence (2003)

Anger Management in Schools: Alternatives to Student Violence, 2nd Edition (2002)

More Hot Stuff to Help Kids Chill Out: The Anger and Stress Management Book (2002)

Case Studies in Rational Emotive Behavior Therapy (2001) with Albert Ellis

Surviving and Thriving in a Blended Family (2000)

Teaching Children Patience Without Losing Yours (1999) with

Polly Wilde

An Educator's Guide to Difficult Parents (1999)

The Subject Is Joy (1998) with John Wilde

Hot Stuff to Help Kids Chill Out: The Anger Management Book (1997)

Treating Anger, Anxiety and Depression in Children and Adolescents: A Cognitive Behavioral Perspective (1996)

Anger Management in Schools: Alternatives to Student Violence (1995)

Rising Above: A Guide to Overcoming Obstacles and Finding Happiness (1995)

Why Kids Struggle in School: A Guide to Overcoming Underachievement (1994)

Rational Counseling with School Aged Populations: A Practical Guide (1992)

In addition to books, Dr. Wilde has written articles appearing in professional journals such as *Elementary School Guidance & Counseling, Anxiety Disorders Practice Journal, Journal of Cognitive Psychotherapy, The Journal of Research in Reading* and *The Journal of Rational-Emotive and Cognitive-Behavior Therapy.*

He and his wife, Polly, live in Richmond, Indiana with their children, Anna and Jack.

JUN 2 1 2010

LaVergne, TN USA
19 April 2010
179763LV00003B/98/P